Me through Us

A Poetry Collection

by: Natalie Colburn

Me Through Us

Copyright © 2023 by Natalie Colburn

All rights reserved.

No part of this publication may be reproduced, distributed, or transmitted in any form or by any means, including but not limited to, photocopying, recording, or other electronic or mechanical methods, without the prior written permission of the publisher except as permitted by U.S. copyright law. For permission requests, contact nataliecolburnwrites@gmail.com.

Written, Designed, and Illustrated by:
Natalie Colburn

Picture Inspiration From: Paul Julian

Natalie Colburn

to us: it would have been a year

Me Through Us

Natalie Colburn

This is a collection of love, of hate, of faith, and of doubt. It contains both joy and sorrow, both optimism and gloom. Both sides of a very real coin.

It tells the story of a girl. She was torn apart but then put back together. Even through the heartbreak, she finds pieces of herself that she never knew existed.

Sure, she lost some, but more importantly, she gained some. So when it's all over, she can, without a doubt, look back and know that it was all God leading her to exactly where she is today. And for that, she couldn't be more grateful.

Me Through Us

Table of Contents

Before us................... pg. 9

Meeting us................ pg. 25

Loving us.................. pg. 37

Destroying us........... pg. 55

Losing us.................. pg. 75

Trusting us............... pg. 93

Me Through Us

Natalie Colburn

Before Us

Me Through Us

Natalie Colburn

Focus

Everyone's Dresses.
Personal Successes.

that's all i'm thinking about

People Projects.
Future Prospects.

that's all i'm focused on

Mimetic Desire.
Perfect Attire.

that's all i'm living for

Me Through Us

Your Residue

I remember...
When you told me I was your queen.

I remember...
From back when I was sixteen.

You were only happy in my Kingdom,
As long as you were my King,
And I couldn't leave the Court.
tied up on a string.

I remember...
When the grass was green.

I remember...
The time we looked all pretty and clean.

But time goes on,
With or Without you.
I no longer need to rely upon,
You and Your residue.

Natalie Colburn

Castle in Ruins

Oh isn't it nice?
living in an illusion.
Until it's gone and shattered
and the castle is in ruin.

Oh isn't it nice?
When the dream ends.

Oh isn't it lovely?
When we no longer pretend.

Oh isn't it nice?
When the dream ends.

Oh isn't it lovely?
When you aren't my friend.

Oh isn't it nice?
living in an illusion.
Until it's gone and shattered
and the castle is in ruin.

Can't Stop Smiling

Today was beautiful.
Today made me feel like I was walking on air.
Today was awesome.
Today made me feel something oh so rare.

Making me wish every day was today
Cause as it is
I Can't Stop Smiling

Today was enchanting.
Today made me feel like dancing forever.
Today was crazy.
Today made me feel no fear whatsoever.

Making me wish every day was today
Cause as it is
I Can't Stop Smiling

Or thinking about you
Or wishing for you
Or hoping
There might be something there

oh well i guess i was wrong

Natalie Colburn

Till the Pain all Goes Away

Even your snide remarks and your little jokes,
Still have my heart beating just a little faster.
No matter how your hair falls,
I still find myself in this disaster.

till the pain all goes away

The voice inside warns me off,
Yelling at what they all consider red flags.
But there's something I cling to,
Ropes made from worn-out rags.

till the pain all goes away

Me Through Us

Cruel

Is there anyone left?
Because the boys nowadays seem so cruel

Offensive jokes are their only love language.
And they only know to speak in rude verbiage.

Vulgar words are all they can manage.
Gosh, they don't even check for the damage.

Lying their way into bed with their fake poise,
Playing with feelings as they play with toys.

With these choices for the future population,
Hope seems gone for the next generation.

Will there be a man left for me?
Because the world is cruel
but a male child is crueler.

Natalie Colburn

I'm Mad.

If only I'd listened to the voice in my head,
Knew you weren't the one for me.
Wishing something instead,
I'm mad.

and now it's embarrassing
thinking through
all the tears I've shed
crying over you

Natalie Colburn

I'm Glad.

Now I hear about how you were falling for her,
Even when you were all over me.
Be it how it were,
I'm glad.

and now it's embarrassing
thinking through
all the tears I've shed
crying over you

Too Much?

Am I just asking for too much?

Someone who will hold me.
When it's cold outside,
when the sun is shining.
That's my only plea.

Someone who's always there.
When the voices get too loud,
when it's all just overwhelming.
That's all, I swear.

maybe i really am asking for too much

Natalie Colburn

Look up

Don't look down,
it's dark over there.

Look up,
breathe in the fresh air.

It's all on you.
It's all in your head.

Switch it up.
Focus on the good instead.

Me Through Us

Natalie Colburn

Waiting

We're all waiting for something.
Be it for . . .
    a second chance or a train to pass

waiting, waiting
tick tock
goes the clock

You may call me impatient,
it is indeed true.
Maybe I'm just complacent,
but Time is a Circle
and Circles never end.

waiting, waiting
tick tock
hurries the clock

We're all waiting for something
Be it for . . .
    a trial to end or a dream to surpass
                  and i'm waiting for us

Me Through Us

Natalie Colburn

Meeting Us

Me Through Us

Natalie Colburn

Prayed for Us

I've never prayed for anything
As much as I have you

The boy of my forever,
I think you might just be.
I ask God every day,
To see if He does agree.

The world says I'm off,
Maybe even a little strange.
But I keep talking to Him,
And everything He does arrange.

I've never prayed for anything
As much as I have us

A List

I never knew I had a list.
My mother always asked,
and I truly thought I didn't.
Now it's begun to be unmasked.

he needs to be warm
like the sun

he needs to be joyful
a bright light

he needs to be gentle
the storm undone

he needs to be sweet
a positive invite

I never knew I had a list.
I mean gorgeous was always a plus,
but meeting you has set the bar.
Now there's no way it adjusts.
                      let's be honest, he needs to be you

Natalie Colburn

Anything & Everything

From the beginning
It's always been blue.
From the teal of the sky
To the turquoise hue.

Sure, it's always been true,
I'm a fan of anything blue.
But more importantly,
I've become a fan of everything you.

So when I saw your hair
Your eyes
I couldn't help but stare.
And if I had said otherwise
They know
It would all be lies.

Territory Unknown

I left you sitting there
and I left you alone.

I promise I wasn't trying
and I really should have known.

I missed the signals
and went off on my own.

I do want to apologize
and promise to atone.

I'm new to this thing called love
and it's all territory unknown.

Natalie Colburn

Reassess

Is this it?
Are you the one?

To see through the mess
My life priorities
Which I know I must reassess

Is this it?
Have you broken the spell?

You shook me awake
Made me realize
All that's at stake

Natalie Colburn

This Thing Called Love

It wasn't until I saw you,
with those wide brown eyes.
They got me seeing things anew.

It wasn't till I heard you,
your smile making me smile.
It was something I wanted to pursue.

It wasn't until I met you,
containing a certain kindness.
You were more than a view.

I realized there was more.
More to this thing called Love.
Than just the pretty words
and the pretty faces.

Be Free

One part of my world gotta give,
in order for the other half to survive.

I can't be living in two lives,
being barely able to survive.

It's not like I can split myself in two,
it's not like how they say it's gonna be.

So I took neither path,
instead choosing to be free.

I choose to be with you,
deciding I'd just rather feel alive.

Natalie Colburn

Me Through Us

Natalie Colburn

Loving Us

Me Through Us

Natalie Colburn

Thank You

Thank You

Thank You for him.
Thank You for placing him in my life.
He's what I've prayed for,
I only hope to one day be his wife.

Thank You for this.
Thank You for answering all my writing.
Of course, you knew,
Exactly what I needed, all on your timing.

Thank You for it all.

Different

My smile feels different.
Brighter. Wider. Lighter.

Being Yours.
Unstoppable. Inaudible. Remarkable.

My life feels so different.
Forever. Better. Together.

Natalie Colburn

Your Scent

Your scent
mingles in a way I can't describe
but let me try

It's the blanket on my bed,
Soft and Warm.
Heavy, but not suffocating.
The best comfort form,
The one we picked together.

It's the sun in the morning,
Hopeful and Bright.
Promising, but not blinding.
The best source of light,
The one I hope to see together.

It's the waves of the oceans,
Beautiful and Arresting.
Powerful, but not destructive.
The best exhilaration testing,
The one I want to experience together.

something I never want to forget

This Side of Me

You bring out this
Unique
Side of Me

Overthinking?
Gone.

You bring out this
Wonderful
Side of Me

Anxiety?
Gone.

You bring out this
Beautiful
Side of Me

Confidence?
Peace?
Here to Stay.

Natalie Colburn

Unforgettable

You're like the water from a flowing river
On a hot summer day
So clear
So refreshing

You're like the wait that's decided to deliver
After years of being away
So anticipated
So desired

You're like the fresh air that makes you shiver
As if I've been drowning
So significant
So unforgettable

Our Adventure

Splashing through the waves
and kicking up the leaves.

I want you on those adventures.

Traveling across the world
and raising kids of our own.

I want you on my adventures.

Late night dances in the rain
and movie nights on the couch.

I can't wait until the adventures become
Our Adventure.

Natalie Colburn

A Room Full of Strangers

In a Room Full of Strangers,
I'd pick you out.
It wouldn't even be hard
Of that I have no doubt.

It's not even a question,
My soul could never forget you.

In a Room Full of Strangers,
You'd always stand out.
Believe me, I would know
We're together. Devout.

Our hearts are pulled together,
By something stronger than I can control.

Natalie Colburn

In a Room Full of Strangers,
You're the one I can't live without.
That's how I'll know
How not to reroute.

Forever will be a string tying us to each other,
One I never want to break.

In a Room Full of Strangers,
You don't count.
Because just so you know,
You could never be a stranger to me.

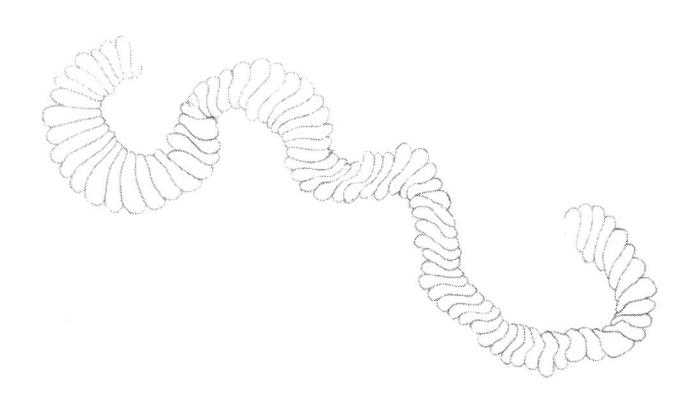

It's Us

It's you and me
It's us
Let's get out of here,
Maybe take a bus.

Till the end of forever,
I won't put up a fuss.
It's you and me
It's us

Natalie Colburn

Peace of Mind

With you
I've found a part of me
And I'll never let her go

She's left behind
All the worry
And all the doubt

A peace of mind
Has settled in
No matter which route

I like this part of me
I don't think I'll be letting go

Me Through Us

Natalie Colburn

Personal Nightlight

Instead of just hoping you are,
I'm going to believe you're right.

You're always telling me to believe,
To keep the end goal in sight.

Maybe that's why I love you so.
You're like my own personal nightlight.

So instead of just hoping you are,
I'm going to believe you're right.

my own personal nightlight

Up and Down

One moment I'm good,
then one I'm not.
I'm sorry I am this way,
I just keep getting caught.

Everything's up and down,
twisting from side to side.
But that's normal right,
a part of the ride.

I'm just grateful I have you,
holding my hand tight.
The dark can't win,
you're keeping me upright.

Natalie Colburn

Pinky Promise

I let myself get carried away.
My mind, like a river, polluted.
It yelled at me, it's hopeless to stay!
But my doubts, all previously disputed.

I forgot that I've already decided,
that nothing can stop us.
So it's pointless to act otherwise.
I've sworn by my pinky promise.

I'm sitting here pretending to do the math.
My heart, like a star, set to implode.
As if I haven't already chosen my path.
Still stuck in my imaginary crossroad.

I've already seen where it ends,
other's may fall apart, but not us.
You and me, together at last.
That's always been my pinky promise.

Me Through Us

Natalie Colburn

Destroying Us

Me Through Us

Natalie Colburn

May I Beg Your Pardon?

Stolen Moments.
Met out in the Garden,
Make us keep it Silent.
May I beg your pardon?

Everybody Else.
You know the Opponents,
Gotta break it Down.
Even the necessary components?

The Threats.
The Rumors.
all fingers pointing.

The Dreams.
The Fantasies.
my bad for disappointing.

Quiet Whispers.
All spoken in the Dark,
Gotta play it Smart.
Have they left a mark?

Unaccommodating Minds.
Want us to go Away,
Got a date with Destiny.
What do you say?

How Can I Help You?

Dull Eyes
Hopeless Sighs
You smile, but it doesn't quite reach your eyes

Hunched Shoulders
Head Bent Low
How can I help you, I just want to know

I know who's killing you.
I know what's silencing your voice.
Just please know that I'll always be here,
As long as I'm given the choice.

Natalie Colburn

Why is it We?

Rules, Regulations, Regimes
Why is it we who have to suffer?

They all just don't get it.
They all just don't understand.
Keeping us apart,
Kinda seems planned.
If this keeps up,
It'll be watching our destruction firsthand.

Punishments, Penalties, Prices
Why is it we who have to suffer?

It seems like there's always something.
It seems like we can't ever catch a break.
Always us running,
Anticipating the ache.
They tell me,
That it all comes down to our own mistake.

Sorrows, Sins, Sentences
Why is it we who have to suffer?

All In Theory

I feel like I might have to leave you behind.
cause the train just keeps coming
nobody there to switch the tracks
I think the whole time, I've just been blind.

It's sad
Cause in theory, we work,
but theory isn't real, honey.
Thinking we won the game,
all while we were losing the money.

I feel like I might have thought too far ahead.
running before the shot went off
not seeing the cliff at the end
I think this whole time, I've been bleeding red.

It's stupid
That in theory, we work,
but what's hypothetical, doesn't last, baby.
Thought we were standing on solid ground,
but now I realize it's always been shaky.

Natalie Colburn

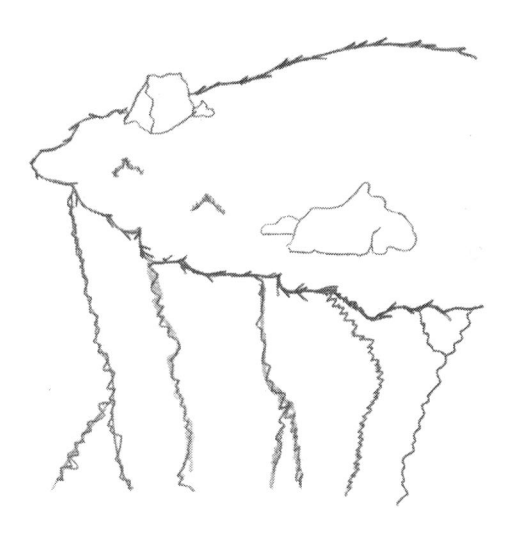

Test Run

i think

in their mind
i am only a test run
something of that kind
you know?

i think

they find it
a trial before full price
something easily quit
am i right?

i think

we feel different
not just playing around with it
more than indifferent
is that true?

Natalie Colburn

I Wish I Could

i'm sorry

i can't keep dancing around
the line dividing us
it's neither of our faults
it is just the way it is

i'm sorry

i can't keep pretending
that nothing is wrong
something needs to happen
an explosion or a miracle

i'm so sorry

i can't change the outcome
even though i wish i could
just some things aren't meant to be
but i really thought we were

Shut My Mouth

Gosh if only I had kept my mouth shut

There wouldn't have been pain
There wouldn't have been punishment

If only I had kept my mouth shut

I've never been great at keeping it in

Burying it so far deep down
That no one can find it

It's all too much for me to keep in

For some people, it's too much to hear

But imagine having to live with it
Every day of your life

Is that too much to hear?

Natalie Colburn

What's Worth Fighting For?

What's worth fighting for?

Surely not
A selfish manipulator
Such as myself

Surely not
The unhealthy person
I certainly am

Surely not
All the plans we made
Now gone

Surely not
What I thought was a consensus
Guess I was wrong

>   *none of it must be worth fighting for*

The Worst Me

I'm becoming what they want
this thing
It's jumbling up my font

I'm angry
I'm bitter
I've gone far off the path

I'm destructive
I'm unregulated
I've jumped off the deep end

I'm doing what I told myself not
this thing
It's turning my heart to rot

this is the worst me

Natalie Colburn

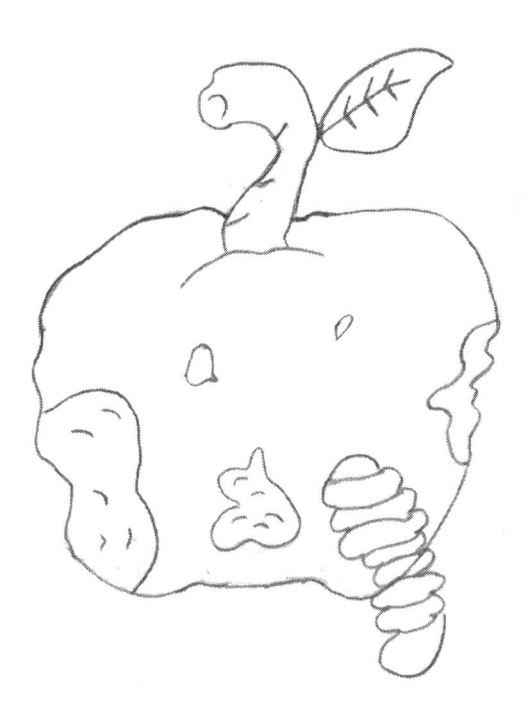

I Thought

What does that say about me,
Can't even wait a couple of years.

There's a part of me, that with them I agree,
I'm not the nice girl like it all appears.

I thought I could change,
Switch up the nasty habit of being impatient.

Maybe the chess board I could rearrange,
Put pieces back in place, perfectly adjacent.

For you, I thought I would do anything.
But I think I might have been lying.

For you, I thought I could do everything.
But I think I underestimated their prying.

Natalie Colburn

The Shredder

Pointless and Unusable
That's what they've decided I am.
Nothing more than a scrap of paper,
Not even worthy to use on an exam.

Irrelevant and Dispensable
That's what they've called me.
Nothing more than a broken record,
Something no one need ever see.

They put me through the shredder.
The only question is.

Will you be able to tape me back together?

Me Through Us

Natalie Colburn

Burning Bridges

There will ALWAYS be a them.

Will next time be any different?

Well,
I guess it appears as though,
That's a challenge for another day.

We'll burn those bridges when we get there.

Write This Down

Write this down, okay?
Don't forget it,
I mean every word,
The verb and the noun.

If you're good enough,
It should be up to me,
It doesn't matter what they think.
Don't you see?

The letters don't matter to me,
I've already claimed you.
It should be my judgment,
Under my review.

You deserve me,
Faults and flaws included.
So don't believe in their lies,
Keep your mind unpolluted.

Write This Down.
Don't forget it.
I mean every word,
The verb and the noun.

i love you.

Natalie Colburn

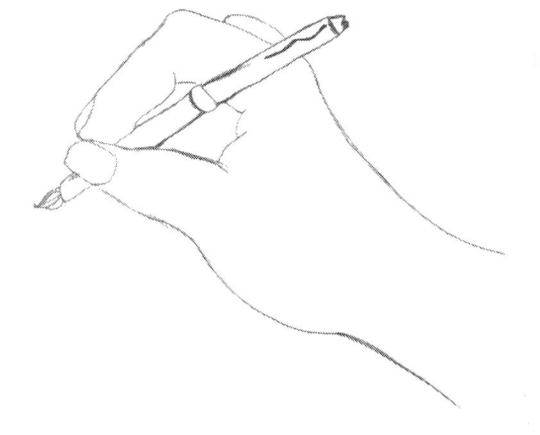

Me Through Us

Natalie Colburn

Losing Us

Me Through Us

Natalie Colburn

A Choice

If I had a choice,
I'd be with you.

If I had a choice,
You'd be with me.

If I had a choice...
I would still talk to you

If I had a choice. . .
I

....

Nevermind.
They took it away.

Go Away

The pain won't go away.

I can't breathe
I can't think

It just won't go away.

i'm missing my other half
it's been torn right out of my chest
by the surgeons who think they're out here
doing good on our behalf

I wish you hadn't been forced to go away.

You helped me breathe
You helped me think

But you were forced to go away.

Natalie Colburn

Desperately

Please please please
don't let us be over

No no no
i don't think i can keep my composure

Desperately.
I want you back.
Desperately.
I wish you were here.

Why why why
have i really lost you forever

No no no
i don't want this whatsoever

Me Through Us

Natalie Colburn

Death By Broken Heart

I know what they mean now
When they say things like
You can feel your heart breaking

it hurts
it's overwhelming
it aches
it's suffocating

So I know what they mean now
When they say stuff like
Heartbreak is an illness

i feel completely drained
it makes me dizzy
i feel nauseous
it makes me sick

I wish I didn't know what they meant
When they told me
You can die from a broken heart

Not Some Teenage Fling

My crying.
My tears.
Aren't all for nothing.

My sorrow.
My pain.
Doesn't come from nowhere.

It's not some
Teenage Fling
Or mutual break
That did this

It's the painful truth
They violently tore me up
And spit me back out
Expecting everything to be normal

Natalie Colburn

Alone

I can laugh and giggle
like nothing's wrong

I can fake a smile
in a crowded room

But as soon as they leave
it doesn't take long

I feel your absence most

alone.

Fireworks

Well, would you look at that?
365 days later and nothing's changed.

Still, we're watching the same show
But from different places.
And in the same sky
It all feels like such a low blow.

I've always loved the colors
But now they leave me lonely.
The sounds of explosions
Remind me of us falling lovers.

It's a different year
But the same feelings.
I just wish you could be with me
I just wish that you could be near.

Well, would you look at that?
365 days later

and everything's changed

Natalie Colburn

Could Be & Should've Been

It's definitely harder
leaving behind
all the could be
and the should've been

there's something missing
living alone
where we could be together
in the house that should've been ours
a beautiful dream
lost in the wind
it really could be here
and it really should've been real
the setting sun
looks very familiar
the light could be shining
and the night should've been denied

It's definitely harder.
leaving behind
what could be my only
and what certainly should've been my forever.

Natalie Colburn

If I Could Be

If I could be
I would be
There in a heartbeat

That's what they don't understand.

If I could be
I would be
Up all night with you

That's what they don't understand.

If I could be
I would be
Not feeling so broken

That's what they don't understand.

Playing Tricks

Even if I move on,
you'll always be,
in the back of my mind.

Playing Tricks,
Keeping me consumed.

I could find someone else,
and you'd still be there,
the forefront of my mind.

Playing Tricks,
Stealing my heart.

There's no one else,
that could pique my interest,
honestly, I don't even mind.

By all means,
keep Playing Tricks.

Natalie Colburn

Green

Going down a deep hole
Remembering all the ways we flew
Every place we used to stroll
Entertain all the fears of you
Not shedding a tear, while I'm out of control

Green was your favorite color art
Right now all it does is remind me of pain
Everything we built together, torn apart
Eventually it was all under too much strain
Never even given a chance from the start

Going to just hope for the end of this pain
Remembering light at the end of the tunnel
Every thought in my overthinking brain
Entertain the dark and despair funnel
Not considering the love that still does remain

Me Through Us

Repetitive, Repeat, Repeating

I feel so repetitive
Always on repeat
Repeating myself
Over and Over

I feel so on repeat
Repeating always
Myself so repetitive
About the Loss

I feel like repeating
Always so repetitive
Myself on repeat
It won't Stop

sorry, i'm not over it

Natalie Colburn

Number One

I lost the only one.
Who's ever placed me up
In spot number one.

I lost the only one.
Who's ever made me
Not the second choice.

Now he's gone.
And I'm left wondering
And I'm left unsure

how do i find value in myself?

Me Through Us

Natalie Colburn

Trusting Us

Me Through Us

Option 3

I move on.
I burn the photos.
I throw it all away.

That would be getting over it.
That would be coping.
That's Option 3.

I let it go.
I stop believing.
I put the bracelet down.

But nothing can stop the memories.
But there's not much hope in that one.
I hate Option 3.
                        let's be honest, it's not really me

Still Stuck

These poor guys,
thinking our separation was mutual.
When instead,
it was anything but considered usual.

How do I break these poor souls?
I wince and I shrink.
I stutter and I overthink.
How do I break it to them?

These poor guys,
Oh, they're in for such a trip.
Because truly,
My heart is still stuck in our relationship.

Natalie Colburn

With You

My heart is still with you.
Even though everyone tells me no.
Even though everyone says I should just let go.
Sorry, I've never been a good listener.

Because I can still feel it.
Pounding in time with yours.
Even from miles apart.
Still, I can feel it.

My heart is still with you.
And unreturned it shall be.
Until the day you're free.
To place it back where it belongs.

Every Now and Again

Every now and again

It hits me so hard.
Please come walk through that door.
although i know you won't

Every now and again

I feel it in my chest.
Please come ease my broken heart.
although i know you can't

Every now and again

I just want you with me.
Please help make them understand.
although i know they don't

is it really that hard to understand?

Natalie Colburn

If It Meant Meeting You

All our memories went from yellow to blue.
But I'd still do it all over
if it meant meeting you.

There's a part of me I've finally met.
She laughs and she jokes,
and she's learned not to fret.

There isn't a second I'd take back.
You've lightened my shoulders,
taking off my loaded pack.

Sure, our memories went from yellow to blue.
But I'd still do it all over
if it meant meeting you.

Natalie Colburn

Ahhhhhh

ahhhhhh

What am I supposed to do?
It's too much pressure,
living without you here.

Ahhhhhhhhhhhh
What am I supposed to do?

Leave the past behind or hold on to the future?

AHHHHHHHHHHHHHHHHHHHHHHHHH

Me Through Us

If You Were Here

I want nothing more than to speak with you

You could give me advice.
except, i know if you were here
i wouldn't even need to wonder

I want nothing more than to hear your voice

The line of them is overwhelming.
except, i know that if you were here
i would just want the one

Natalie Colburn

Again

You probably expect me to live again,
So I will.

You probably expect me to care again,
So I will.

You probably expect me to laugh again,
So I will.

You probably expect me to love again
Too bad.

What I Hope For

I hope.

You're at the end of the tunnel,
with arms wide open.
Even though between us,
there is so much left unspoken.

I believe.

You've left an unremovable stain,
permanent on my heart.
I'll never be able to forget your love,
despite the time that keeps us apart.

I want.

You to be the one,
the one I see with the sunrise.
To never let you go,
and for that, I sincerely apologize.

Natalie Colburn

Maybe Someday

I'm counting down the days until
That Maybe Someday

When I get to see
your smile again.

When I get to hear
your laugh again.

When I get to feel
your arms again.

I'm counting down the days until
That Pesky Maybe Someday

What Ifs

What if I had been better and nice?

What if you had grown a spine?

What if this is exactly where God want us?

What if this is His design?

Natalie Colburn

On My Own

Finding who I am
On My Own.
That's what I've been called to do.

Believing in myself
On My Own.
Without you or anyone around.

Trusting is Hard

I know I need to trust,
but trusting is so hard for my soul.

I know He's got this,
but I find myself still wanting control.

I have to let Him take over,
let Him fight my battles.

I know I need to trust,
but my faith, it rattles.

I don't need to worry,
for You've already won the war.

Please help me to trust,
You've got the best plan in store.

Natalie Colburn

Part of My Journey

Thank You again.

You are my true foundation.
Never moving, always there.

You are my salvation.
Never absent, always protecting.

After time and space,
now I realize.
You were and are still,
putting my life into place.

You are my final destination.
Never failing, always rewarding.

You are the only medication.
Never harming, always healing.

After grace and mercy,
now I see.
It was all necessary,
a part of my journey.

So thank You for it all.

Still Standing Tall

Loneliness is different from being alone.

I've been battered, beaten, and thrown.

Still, here I am, still standing tall.

Only because He is with me through it all.

Natalie Colburn

Next Time

I'll use this time wisely I think.

work on myself
build my knowledge
deepen the relationship
construct our cottage

I hope you use this time wisely.

grow into yourself
don't give in
learn to speak
most importantly when

Maybe then, we'll both be prepared,
prepared for next time.

Natalie Colburn

Future Us

I've never believed in,
right guy, wrong time.
But I suppose this,
this was exactly our crime.

But the right time,
can still occur.
I'll be sitting here,
because you are who I prefer.

I hope we meet again,
and iron out the wrinkle.
I hope there's a future us,
that the you to come is single.

Me Through Us

Natalie Colburn

Let's Do This Thing!

Of course, I remember the date.
But until then,
All that's left to do is wait.

It'll feel like an eternity.
Yet I'm sure,
Together we'll survive this absurdity.

We're in for quite the wild ride.
Better buckle in,
Even though I fully trust our Guide.

Alright.
Are you ready?
Let's Do This Thing!

Me Through Us

Acknowledgments

I don't even know where to start here! I feel like there are so many people who have made this poetry collection possible, there's no way I could list them all. But I'm certainly going to try.

First on the list has to be my family. Neither my parents nor my siblings have ever once doubted me and never once have they discouraged me from accomplishing the things I put my mind to.

Then, to my longest and bestest friend, Gracie. She was the first one to read the entire collection of poetry all laid out in order! We may live far apart but we've known each other for what feels like forever. She has never once been hesitant to hear about what new project I'm trying and is always ready with an encouraging word or piece of advice.

Thank you to all of my many friends and other family members who have offered me so much support in one of the most difficult seasons of my life. They kept me sane and without many of them, I would most definitely be in a much darker place.

Here's a shoutout to all of my ARC readers! They were so awesome, giving me so much support, and every time they made a comment or a post, it would make my day!

Also, a huge thank you to all of you guys for reading this! I'm hoping everyone is able to find hope in these poems, even amidst the not-so-hopeful parts. It's important to remember that everyone faces different and unique challenges, but at the end of the day, they all point us back to God

Most importantly, I owe all of this and who I am to God. He has taught me so many valuable lessons through a time in my life in which I have experienced loss after loss. Yet, He's always reminding me to have hope and place my faith and Him and His perfect plan for my future. Using the struggles I've faced, He's placed a feeling of unbeatable peace and joy in my heart.

The Author

Natalie Colburn is from Arizona whose childhood "side dream" was always writing and publishing her very own book. She vividly remembers the first story she started writing being about a frog going on adventures.

Equal to her love of writing is her love of reading. The only real thing she ever got in trouble for at school was reading instead of doing her work.

Instagram: @nataliecolburnwrites
Email: nataliecolburnwrites@gmail.com

Made in the USA
Columbia, SC
13 March 2024